G0C0020077

instant
meditations

Illustrations by Stéphane Denis

RUNNING PRESS
PHILADELPHIA · LONDON

A Running Press® Miniature Edition™
Copyright © 2002 by Running Press
Illustrations © 2002 by Stéphane Denis
Printed in China

ISBN 0-7624-1363-8

This book may be ordered by email from the publisher. Please add
$1.00 for postage and handling. *But try your bookstore first!*

Running Press Book Publishers
125 South Twenty-second street
Philadelphia, Pennsylvania 19103-4399

Visit us on the web!
www.runningpress.com

Contents

Introduction

"In the fast pace of today's world, there is a growing need to reconnect to the **sacred elements of life.**"

—Denise Linn in *Altars: Bringing Sacred Spaces Into Your Everday Life*

Hidden deep within each of us, hidden even from ourselves, is a deep wellspring of power, passion, love, creativity, and fulfillment. This secret part of ourselves has unlimited ability to dream beautiful dreams and make them manifest in our lives.

Within each of us is a pure flame, a spark of the Divine. But it is covered over by the body, and by our habits of mind, even as we cover our

own bodies when we dress. This flame is the source of that magical wellspring within.

Meditation is what feeds the flame. Think of each meditation as a log you throw onto the fire of your soul so it can blaze brighter. If you throw small little logs sporadically, you won't have much of a fire. But if you continue to feed the fire every day, with fresh logs of concentration, meditation and reflection, you will feed that part of yourself most capable of creating exactly the life you want. The longer the meditation, the bigger the log, the brighter the flame.

Often, when we feel stress, the real source is the gap between the conditions in our life and what this deeper part of us—the spark of the Divine—knows we could have.

Often, especially when our self-esteem is low, or we have been taught not to expect much out of life, we settle for a far more colorless, unsatisfying existence than we could have. We make less than productive choices and keep ourselves trapped in cycles of frustration. But meditation puts us in touch with that active dynamic power in ourselves that knows how to attract to us just

what we need, in any moment,
to feel complete contentment.
Because there is a dynamic intelligence within this inner flame, the
very intelligence of the Creator who
made us, by tuning in through
meditation, we can know in any
moment the exact next step to take.
This, in turn, can help us overcome
self-esteem problems, money or
health problems or any kind of

problems at all. Through meditation, we receive the inspiration, the clarity and the answers we need to create complete fulfillment in every sphere of our lives. It even helps make us impervious to stress. Because it awakens the peace already within us, it's easier to let the small stuff go, and harder for anything to get us rattled and off-balance.

The Essence of
Meditation

At its simplest, meditation is communion with that aspect of yourself that still lives in God. Yes, it is there inside of you, but it is a magical part that has never—and will never—be separated from the Creator. Members of some faiths call this aspect the "soul." Other faiths have other names for it. In yogic traditions, it is believed that the seat of the soul is deep within the upper

region of the brain, just behind
that part of the forehead where you
sometimes see Indian women
wearing bindis, or jewels. That's
where yogis place their attention
there when they meditate.

Although meditation may seem
exotic, there is nothing more natural.
Babies do it. When they put all of
their concentration on something,
and bubble with joyous laughter,

they are in contact with that pure joy that is an eternal quality of the soul. Even cats meditate. You know how they sometimes look as if they are staring into the distance, and seem withdrawn inside themselves? What they are doing is akin to meditation. It is a way that they replenish themselves.

"You cannot know [God]
by reading a book about divine
love and joy. Though spiritual
writings do inspire fervor
and faith, they do not give
the end result . . .You must sit
quietly in deep meditation,
if even for just a few minutes

per day, taking the mind away from all else and **focusing** on God alone. Thereby you gradually come to know Him, and knowing Him, you cannot help but love Him."

—Sri Dya Mata in *Enter The Quiet Heart*

The Basic Elements of Meditation

There are many styles of meditation. Later in this book, we'll talk about how to find the style that's just right for you, the one that will feel so perfect for you you'll find it easy to stick with it. Know, however, that all styles of meditation have essentially the same elements. All good meditation practices:

1. Still the mind so that you can clear your thoughts and drop into that deeper part of yourself.

2. Intensify your concentration so you can behold the soul with a steadier gaze. Bringing your attention to your soul opens you to an aspect of yourself which is powerful,

creative and eternal.

3. Deeply relax you so you can open to the nourishment and wisdom of your soul.

4. Provide you with a way to unite breath and mind so that you can go beyond either, to that timeless part of yourself that continues to exist even after you've thought your last thought and breathed your last breath. Even short meditations can

bring you a glimpse of paradise now. Deep and sustained meditation can make your life deeply satisfying and downright magical.

Once you still the mind, relax into your being, unite breath and mind until both seem to fall away, you will be in the magic zone. That is where all of the answers to life's questions can be found. In this still place, you can put forth any question

or a problem, and receive infallible counsel.

Those who practice meditation regularly know this to be true. They have experienced for themselves how meditation has been able to help them overcome the challenges in their lives, and create fulfillment. They've come to count on the guidance they get after a deep meditation. Each of the techniques I will share

"Go deep into yourself and find that way of using your mind and living your life in **peace and harmony** with yourself and the ten thousand things."

—Zen Mountain Monastery Abbot John Daido Loori in *The Heart of Being*

with you in the following pages can
help you do the same. The trick is to
do them regularly, at least once a
day, preferably twice. Start out with
just five minutes and then, as you
can, increase to at least 20. You will
love the changes that you see.

Getting into the 'Zone'

God knows it is hard to stop thinking, especially for those of us who work with our minds everyday. (Those who work with their hands seem to have an easier time of it.) But it is only by stilling our thoughts that we can drop deeply into the 'zone' of meditation. In that state,

you feel absolute peace.

While it is easier to concentrate if you meditate with a group, that's not a requirement. It may help to set aside a place you use only for meditation—say a corner of the bedroom or an alcove. This way, your mind becomes conditioned to quieting down in that space.

Stilling the Mind–Five Techniques

One excellent way to still the mind is to focus exclusively on your breath. This next meditation technique is especially effective at quieting down the mind:

Meditation
EXERCISE #1

Sit and relax. Let your hands come to rest on your lap at the juncture of your hips and thighs. Let your palms be turned upwards in a gesture of receptivity. Now close your eyes and focus your awareness at the point between the eyebrows. Take a deep breath and expel it.

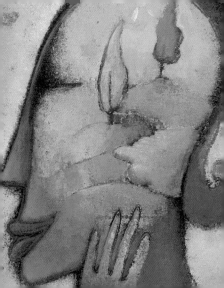

That can help release the toxins in your blood that could make your mind restless. Take another deep breath and expel it, and then another.

Then allow yourself to deeply relax. With your attention still focused upward, at the point between the eyebrows (parallel to the seat of the soul), breathe in for a count of 20, or less if you can't do it for that long of a count. Pretend that

you are drawing your breath up to
that point between the eyebrows.
Then retain your breath for the same
count as your in-breath. Finally,
expel your breath for the same
count. Continue this rhythm of
breathing in up to a count of 20,
holding the breath up to a count of
20, and exhaling up to a count of 20.
You will find it can quickly counter-
act any negative thoughts or anxiety.

This is a basic yoga-style meditation.

In *Meditation as Medicine: Activating the Power of Your Natural Healing Force*, Dr. Dharma Singh Khalsa calls this 20-20-20 breathing the "one-minute breath." He says it is "sometimes called the one-minute cure, because of its unique ability to change a negative thought, feeling or vibration into a positive one." He says this breathing technique can:

- Increase calmness and peace
- Increase creativity and intuition
- Increase cognitive energy
  by increasing blood flow to
  the brain
- Even heighten sexual energy

This 20-20-20 breathing technique is ancient and has been used by sages who teach meditation. Paramahansa Yogananda, author of

Autobiography of a Yogi, a bestseller that has been translated into many languages and is still in print, recommends 20-20 breathing as part of the preparation for a deep meditation.

If Zen is more to your liking than Yoga, here's a basic meditation technique to try:

Meditation
EXERCISE #2

Sit on a pillow or a meditation bench. Let your gaze focus softly on the ground in front of you. Bring your hands to your navel. Hold them in such a way that the fingers of one hand are resting in the palm of the other. Let your thumbnails just touch. Make sure your thumbnails remain that way. The point of this is to keep you alert through the meditation so your mind is less likely to wander. What follows is a basic Zen meditation.

First, breathe in and mentally count "1." On the out-breath, mentally count "2." Continue in this way, counting "3" on the in-breath and "4" on the out-breath, etc., until you reach "10." Then begin the count again at "1." If you remain mindful, you will gradually unite breath and mind. If you let your mind wander, you may find yourself counting to 350 before you catch yourself. That's okay. Just start again. This technique can help you master the mind, which puts you in control, instead of at its mercy.

Meditation
EXERCISE #3

Another way to still the mind and unite mind with breath is to concentrate on a sound, as you do in the following exercise.

Allow yourself to become quiet. Settle into your chair. Notice your feet on the floor. Feel how the earth supports you. Feel how your back is

supported by the chair in which you are sitting. Bring your attention to the breath. Notice how your breath is always with you. (In Hebrew, the word for breath and spirit are the same.) Notice how effortlessly the breath flows, bringing in what is fresh and new, and letting go of what is old and used up.

As you notice your breath, observe the space between the out-

"Zen means to be intimate with the self. To be intimate with the self is to realize the whole phenomenal universe as Self."

—Zen Mountain Monastery Abbot John Daido Loori in *The Heart of Being* breath and the in-breath. At the end of the out-breath, before the in-breath begins, there is a place of complete rest. In that place of complete rest, you can not only you appreciate the peace you feel, but also feel your wholeness.

The word "Shalom" means peace and wholeness. You can meditate on this word by mentally repeating "Sha" on the in-breath and

"Lom" on the out-breath. Repeat until you feel deeply calm and relaxed. If you prefer, you can say "Sha" and "Lom" quietly to yourself as you synchronize the syllables with your breath. This will take you to a deep state of relaxation. Alternately, you can use the word "Amen." Say "Ah"" on the in-breath and "men" on the out-breath. Repeat again and again, until breath and mind become one.

If you would like to have a really deep meditation, first take the time to completely relax before you focus on your breath and repeat the sound of "Shalom." Relaxation is to meditation what stretching is to exercise; in other words, it's a helpful warm-up.

Meditation
EXERCISE #4

A very quick way to use sound to help you focus in meditation is to get a hold of a Zen bell, or a metal or glass Tibetan bowl. Sit quietly, strike the bell and let your mind follow the circular currents of sound as they expand throughout the room. Try hitting the bowl seven times,

feeling the sound first at the base of your spine, then in your pelvis, then in your solar plexus area, then in your heart, then at the base of your throat and neck, then just above the eyebrows and finally, in the crown of your head. Feel these energy centers expand outward, in circles, just like the sound.

If you'd like to experiment with the sound, try taking the wooden

gong that comes with the Zen or
Tibetan bell and circling the edge
of the bell. If you do it just right,
you will produce a mystical sound
that will become louder the more
you press the gong around the outer
edges of the bell. Just this sound
alone can often bring peace. Usually
these bells are made by monks who
pray intensely as they work.

Meditation
EXERCISE #5

This next technique also uses sound. It comes from Sufism, the mystical branch of Islam. This exercise is a bit more complicated because it involves a technique known as "alternate nostril breathing"—which can synchronize the hemispheres of your brain, opening you to greater creativity and wisdom. At the same time, it is deeply relaxing and balancing. The intention behind this meditation is to affirm your oneness with God, and to remember that the only part of you that really exists is that part that is alive in God.

Sit comfortably. You might choose to sit cross-legged on the floor, on a chair with a straight back, or on a meditation bench. Keep your spine straight. Raise your right hand to your face, with the palm flat and facing left. Press your pinky on the left nostril to close it. Draw your breath up through the right nostril. As you do, mentally chant "Alla-Hu" which means "only God exists." Let the breath come to a complete stop. Then remove your pinky and block off the right nostril with your thumb. As you exhale, mentally chant "La il la ha," which means, "nothing exists other than the God." By repeating this over and over again, you identify your consciousness with that which is most Divine in you and free yourself from the unconscious fetters that can disrupt your inner peace.

Meditations that employ sound are very powerful. In fact, ancient Vedic seers believe that when God

created the universe, He willed light and sound to come forth out of himself. That is why the "OM" sound, said to be the vibration behind creation, is considered so powerful. So simply striking a Zen meditation bell or a Tibetan bowl and chanting OM as you hear the sound waves flow outward can put you into the zone, too.

Other Styles of Meditation— Three Techniques

Again, there are many styles of meditation. You are not just limited to using sound to still the mind. You can also use visualization or even movement. The trick is to pick something that feels good to you.

As long as the practice contains the basic elements already discussed, it will take you where you need to go.

To determine the kind of meditation that's right for you, take a moment to think about your dominant sense. Are you a highly visual person? Then a visual meditation might work best for you. Do you love music and sound? Then a sound-based meditation might be

most effective. Are you active,
dynamic, or kinesthetically sensitive?
Then you might benefit from a
movement or walking meditation.

Meditation
EXERCISE #6

Light a candle. Gaze intently at the blue center of the flame. Gaze so intently that you memorize everything about it: its shape, its color, its intensity, the way it move. Focus on it—to the sole exclusion of everything else—for at least three to five minutes. You want to know it so

intimately, then when you close your eyes, you can still see the image of the flame in your mind with your eyes closed. Place that image in the area of your third eye, which is slightly above the area on your forehead where your eyebrows part. As you recreate the image with your eyes closed, do so with the intention that you're gazing on the radiant inner flame within you. Look lov-

ingly upon this flame in your mind's
eye, and know that as you "feed" it
with conscious attention, you are
reuniting with your soul and its
timeless, ever-relevant wisdom.

Meditation
EXERCISE #7

Tai Chi, Chi Gung, and even Zen walking meditation are all forms of movement-oriented meditations. Even walking can be a meditation. The story is told, for instance, about how one Nigerian tribal elder used his morning walk to his farm as a walking meditation.

He'd rise with the sun, dress very simply, throw over his shoulder a horsetail for swatting flies and start his walk. As he walked, he would look straight down the road, neither left nor right. He would take care to move at just the right pace, so he could align his body, mind and spirit. If he needed to swat flies, he would; otherwise he was totally focused on taking the next step for-

ward. This practice can make it easier
to move toward goals with complete
focus, and is especially good for peo-
ple who are easily distracted.

You can adapt this for yourself
by setting the intention to walk in
alignment with your spirit, and to
keep moving ahead. As you walk,
notice how your feet make contact
with the ground. Allow your arms to
swing in a way that feels natural to

you. Slow down, allow your entire being to align and walk ahead with purpose. Let your thoughts go and focus on feeling your body as it moves through space. Let your breath synchronize with your movements. Feel the peace of moving at your own natural pace, neither being ahead of yourself, or so "in your head" that you are not aware of your body.

Another variation to try is this standing meditation, loosely based on Taoism and T'ai Chi. This is a great one to do out of doors, where you can put your bare feet on the earth. It's also useful if you want to practice in the office, and don't have a lot of space. With this meditation, unlike the others where you close your eyes, no one can accuse you of sleeping on the job!

Meditation
EXERCISE #8

If you prefer to do a standing meditation in the Taoist style, here is a
good one. This is best practiced out-
side on the earth, in bare feet, but
you can also do it indoors with socks
on. Begin by standing with your feet
shoulder width apart. Let your knees
be loose. Sink down, as if you were

"What joy such a soul receives
who sees herself so sweetly
arrived at this pass, for in truth
she tastes the happiness of the
angelic nature."

—St. Catherine of Sienna

riding on a horse. Let your focus drop into your belly or your solar plexus area. Now bring your hands together and rub them briskly. Do so until you feel the heat emanating from your palms. Bring your hands together and apart, and together and apart, until you can feel the ball of energy between them. This is called chi, and it is a concrete expression of your life energy. Keep building this

chi by bringing your hands together
and apart. Imagine that you are
drawing up energy from the earth
through your feet, and drawing it up
your legs, into your abdomen and
back, up your chest and into your
arms. Feel that the "earth" chi is
blending with your own energy, and
making the ball of electricity
between your hands even larger.
When it feels large enough, put your

hands on your abdomen, visualize the chi entering the center of your body and getting larger and larger until the circle completely engulfs you. Let yourself melt into the sweetness of your own expanded life force, as you breathe in energy from every corner of the universe.

Invocation Style Meditations

Often, just by concentrating on a particular figure of greatness, whether spiritual or secular, you can enter into their consciousness and elevate your own mind. These next meditations work on that principle.

Meditation
EXERCISE #9

Sometimes, you can drop more easily into the zone by invoking a spiritual figure who has great meaning to you. If you are a Christian, you may want to visualize Christ or his mother, Mary, or your favorite saint. If you are Jewish, you might want to imagine G-D, or Sophia. If

you are Hindu, you might want to
visualize Krishna, or Shiva, Durga,
Saraswati, or Lakshmi. If you are
Buddhist, you might want to
visualize Buddha in one of his many
aspects, or Tara. If you resonate with
the Goddess religions, consider
calling on Kwan Yin, Isis, Ishtar,
Artemis/Diana, Aphrodite, Athena,
Hera, or Hecate. If you are Native
American, you might want to invoke

The Great Spirit or White Buffalo
Woman. The important thing is to
choose a spiritual figure who means
a great deal to you.

You can do this meditation
sitting or standing. It helps to have
a quiet place where you feel comfortable closing your eyes. Take the
time to relax your body, then let your
focus come into your heart. Imagine
that you have lips in your heart, and

use those lips to mentally call upon
your spiritual figure. Ask them to
come into your heart. Keep calling
until you feel the presence of that
very special being. Ask for their
blessing. Ask for your hearts to
merge. Ask for the grace to invoke
their energy any time you need it.

Meditation
EXERCISE #10

For women, it can be very empowering to invoke the female form of the Divine. The Goddess is known by many names, in many different cultures. And in each of those cultures, there might be animals, or other objects associated with the Goddess. For instance, the Greek

goddess Diana, the Huntress, is often seen with a bow and arrow and a greyhound. The goddess Athena is often depicted with an owl. You can invoke the Goddess by calling on an aspect that is familiar to you, or by calling on an aspect that has some quality you need. If you want to become more powerful in business, for instance, call on Athena. You might want to read about her first, perhaps in Jean Shinoda Bolen's book, *Goddesses in Every Woman,* or do some Web research. Then create an altar with objects sacred to Athena. To invoke Athena you might put a small stuffed owl, a replica of the Greek-style scale, plus a candle. If you want to invoke Aphrodite, the goddess of love, you might put beautiful shells and three golden apples upon your altar. Here

are examples of other aspects of the
Goddess you could invoke:

For wisdom—*Sofia*

For healing—*Isis, the White Tara, Inana,
White Buffalo Woman*

For Compassion—*Kwan Yin, Durga, Tara*

For help in childbirth—*Diana*

For love—*Aphrodite*

For prosperity—*Athena, Lakshmi*

For greater creativity—*Brigit, Changing
Woman*

For transformation—*Demeter and Persephone*

For spiritual awakening—*Isis, Kali, Durga, Tara*

Meditation
EXERCISE #11

This meditation uses visualization
and it invokes the presence of a
spiritual being. To do it, find a
mandala, a sacred image that often
incorporates a spiritual figure, like a
Buddha, or Kali. (You can find these
on silk in the kinds of stores that sell
incense or religious artifacts.)

Buddhist mandalas usually feature a Buddha or the goddess Tara, considered a symbol of Divine Compassion. Hindu mandalas may contain illustrations of the Hindu pantheon of gods, such as Kali or Shiva. Find one that appeals to you.

When you are ready to do your mandala meditation, take the time to relax deeply. Try tensing every muscle group in your body from your

toes to the top of your head. Then
sit in a comfortable position with
the mandala in front of you. Gaze
so intently at it that you memorize
it. Focus on it until you can recreate
it in your mind's eye. Allow yourself
to merge with the spiritual figure
depicted on the mandala. This can
alter your state of mind and make
you receptive to higher wisdom.

Meditation
EXERCISE #12

If you are feeling out of sorts, or your mind is spinning on a particular subject and you know you need to stop obsessing about what is driving you crazy, this exercise is just the ticket. You can use it to go from feeling lousy to fantastic in practically no time. It will bring you greater

self-awareness and a sense of well-being. It is based on a self-awareness technique, called Focusing, which was developed by Eugene Gendlin at the University of Chicago. Focusing has adherents around the world, and is often used to compliment—or as a substitute for—psychotherapy. You can do it alone, or with a partner, with each person taking turns.

Here is a focusing exercise for you to try by yourself.

Take a moment to really relax. Tense and release each of your muscles. Loosen any tight clothing. When you feel really relaxed, take a moment to be very present with yourself in your body. Notice how your feet touch the ground. Notice the places where your body touches the back of the chair, the seat of the chair. Bring your awareness of yourself into your body, down from your head, into your solar plexus.

Then use your mind to scan your body.

Is there some part of you that's calling your attention? Maybe something that really stands out, like a fluttering in the belly or tightness at the nape of your neck.

Whatever it is, let your attention "pause" at that part of you.

Be very attentive to the sensa-tions in that part of your body. Do your best to describe what it feels like. For instance, if the neck feels tight, you might acknowledge to yourself: "Neck feels tight. It feels like there's a cord drawn tightly there." Just noticing the "cord" will help it loosen.

Continue to "hold" that area of

your body with loving awareness.
Ask it what it is about the tightness
that you don't yet know. Then
remain quiet until the body floats
an answer to the surface of your
consciousness. You may 'hear' your
inner voice clueing you in as to what
the tension is really about, or you
may feel a flood of tears about some
situation that you haven't completely
resolved. Let them come. With

them, will come a melting of the tension. Essentially, once you pay attention, you allow your body to transfer the "information" in the tension to a thought, such as, 'I need to set a better boundary and not always volunteer my services" or into a feeling, such as the hurt that produces tears. In this way, you facilitate an "internal housecleaning" that removes anything that stands

"Focusing is . . .

more than being in touch with your feelings and different from body work. [It] occurs exactly at the interface of body-mind [and] consists of specific steps for getting a body sense of how you are in a particular life situation. The body sense is unclear and vague at first, but if you pay attention it will open up into words or images and you experience a felt shift in your body. In the process of Focusing, one experiences a physical change in the way that the issue is being lived in the body. We learn to live in a deeper place than just thoughts or feelings. The whole issue looks different and new solutions arise."

—From the Focusing Institute

between you and your well being.

Focusing can be used to help you take the next positive step in your relationships, in your work and in your spiritual development. Even a few minutes spent on Focusing each day can make a big difference.

Meditation
EXERCISE #13

Here's a naturalistic, shamanistic approach to meditation, one that will allow you to feel freer in your life. It is also useful if you want to bring forth a special desire, whether that's achieving a particular goal or manifesting a relationship.

Begin by going out in nature

where you can find bird feathers. Places where hawks circle, or woods filled with the songs of birds, would be a good place to look.

Once you gather your feathers, set up an altar with incense and any objects you consider sacred. Set the feathers·on your lap. Then begin breathing in a steady rhythmic way to help you relax. Try breathing in for a count of six, holding for six,

"A very ancient pagan ritual involves placing a knife into a cup, symbolizing the union of the Father and Mother. This is an act of creation. Every time you place a prayer stick into a fetish bowl, you are symbolically doing

the same thing. Anytime male
and female unite, whether
sexually or symbolically, there
is a birth of new
energy expressions."

—Ted Andrews in *Animal-Speak*

then exhaling for six. Feel yourself relaxing more with each and every breath.

Then bring to mind the image of the bird whose feathers you are holding. Visualize it in flight. See its qualities radiating within your mind and experience the freedom you would feel if you were soaring in flight, just as the bird is. Then pick up the feather. Imagine how the birds' wings move in flight. Inhale as the wings move up; exhale onto the feather as the wings you're imagining move down. Completely merge with your image of the soaring bird. You may feel the feather begin to vibrate. If so, imagine that energy moving into your body. Then imagine yourself successfully using these newfound abilities to fly and soar and swoop down on opportunities, in the coming weeks. If you'd like to manifest something in particular, use the feather to make a prayer stick and then place the prayer stick in a clay fetish bowl.

To do this, attach a feather to a tree branch, such as a willow. You can peel, notch, or paint the branch. According to Ted Andrews, author of *Animal-Speak,* the Hopi and Pueblo Indians considered such prayer sticks "the most important tool for connecting with and making offerings and petitions to the spirit world." When you make your prayer stick, breathe gently through the feather onto the stick activate its energy. Then fill the bowl with quartz crystal points or sacred stones, and implant the prayer stick.

Meditation
EXERCISE #14

The thirteen preceding exercises
have been drawn from yoga, Zen
Buddhism, Judaism, Tibetan
Buddhism, Sufism, African tribal
traditions, Taoism, mystical
Christianity, the Goddess religions,
transpersonal psychology, and
shamanism. Each of these medita-

tions can take you into the zone. Once you've tried each of them once—if you're so inclined—let yourself return to the one that most appeals to you. You might even find you want to explore that tradition more thoroughly and learn advanced techniques.

Whatever meditation style you chose, the important thing is to stick with it so you can go deep. If you take the time to practice regularly, you will feel tremendous peace. Regular practice will also open to you the miraculous region of your soul, that place where you can float any question that is troubling you, any problem that is bothering you, and receive back wise counsel that is meant for you alone.

Just be aware that you don't have to confine your "instant meditations" to isolated moments of practice. The Buddhist practice of mindfulness, particularly as it is taught by a saintly Vietnamese monk by the name of Thich Nat Hahn, can help you to live moment-to-moment in that meditative state of contentment and expanded awareness. Thich Nat Hahn teaches very simple breathing techniques where you pay attention to what you

"Wherever you are you can **breathe mindfully.** We all need to go back to ourselves from time to time in order to confront the difficulties of life. . .one time, I was waiting for an airplane that was four hours late at Kennedy Airport in New York, and I enjoyed sitting cross-legged in the waiting area . . ."

—Thich Nat Hahn in *Peace in Every Step: The Path of Mindfulness in Everyday Life* are doing. For instance, you can think to yourself as you are breathing, "Breathing in, I breathe in peace. Breathing out, I let go of stress. Breathing in, I breathe in peace. Breathing out, I let go of stress." If you were to repeat this for just five moments, remaining aware of your in-breath as you breathe in, and your out-breath as you breathe out, you could quickly calm yourself.

Try it. You will see.

Be well,
and be at peace.

This book has been bound using
handcraft methods and Smyth-sewn
to ensure durability.

The package, book cover, and interior
were designed by Gwen Galeone.

Illustrations by Stéphane Denis.

The text was written and edited
by Deborah Grandinetti.

The text was set in ACaslon,
Univers, and Aperto.